Tuning In

This book is a recount and is best read from [...] first. However, when they have finished the [...] may choose to reread the parts they found [...]

CW00673167

Start by reading pages 2–3 with the group and then ask the children to continue on their own. Ask them to skim through the book and find three main headings and an example of a diagram and a chart.

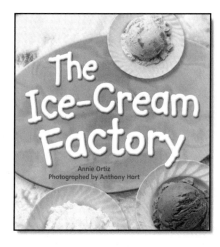

The front cover

Let's read the title – what is the book about?

Do you like ice-cream? Would you like to know how it is made?

The back cover

Why did the children visit the ice-cream factory?

Would you like to visit one?

What is your favourite flavour of ice-cream?

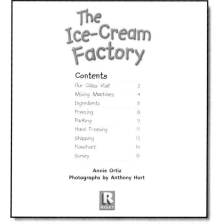

Contents

Look at the contents. Can you see the words 'ingredients', 'flowchart', 'survey'?

What do you think they mean?

Read pages 2 and 3

Purpose: to look at the structure of a recount,

to understand why the class went round the ice-cream factory.

Pause at page 3

Why do you think the children chose to visit an ice-cream factory?

Why do you think the pages look like a notebook?

Why do you think they have photographs and drawings?

Let's look at the text by the arrow. How much milk is brought to the factory?

What do you think is the main ingredient of ice-cream?

Our Class Visit

Do you ever wonder how some things are made? Our class wondered how ice cream, our favourite dessert, is made. So we made a trip to an ice-cream factory to find out!

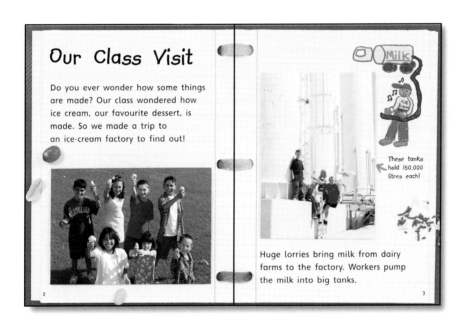

These tanks hold 150,000 litres each!

Huge lorries bring milk from dairy farms to the factory. Workers pump the milk into big tanks.

Milk

2

3

READ

Read pages 4 and 5

Purpose: to use diagrams and illustrations to retrieve
        information.

EXPLORE

Pause at page 5

Look at the drawing on page 4. What does it tell us?

Why do you think the people in the photographs are
wearing hair nets?

What happens to the milk after it has been heated?

Mixing Machines

The first machine heats the milk to kill any germs. We didn't know milk had 80°C germs! Then another machine mixes the heated milk until it's smooth and thick.

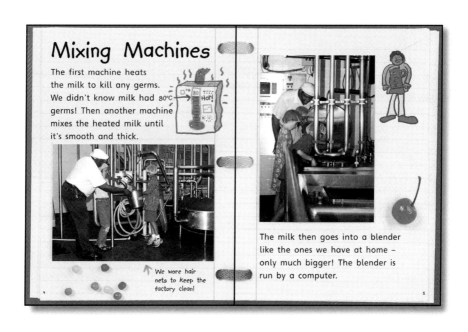

↑ We wore hair nets to keep the factory clean!

The milk then goes into a blender like the ones we have at home – only much bigger! The blender is run by a computer.

5

READ

Read pages 6 and 7

Purpose: to read the text and the illustrations together.

EXPLORE

Pause at page 7

What does the title say on this page?

What do you think is added to the milk?

Who can see a list? Would you like to read it aloud?

Why is there a drawing of a strawberry, a peach and a banana on page 7?

Now read the text on your own and find out where the flavouring is kept.

Let's work out what ingredients go into making ice-cream.

Tricky word (page 6):
The word 'delicious' may be beyond the children's word recognition skills. Tell this word to the children.

Ingredients

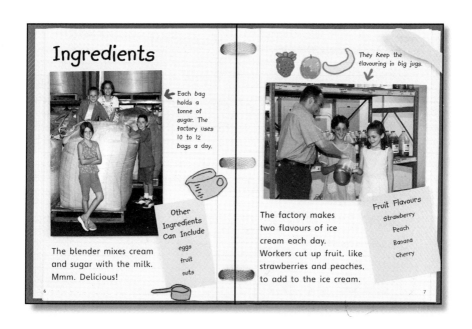

Each bag holds a tonne of sugar. The factory uses 10 to 12 bags a day.

They keep the flavouring in big jugs.

Other Ingredients Can Include

eggs

fruit

nuts

The blender mixes cream and sugar with the milk. Mmm. Delicious!

The factory makes two flavours of ice cream each day. Workers cut up fruit, like strawberries and peaches, to add to the ice cream.

Fruit Flavours

Strawberry

Peach

Banana

Cherry

6

7

READ

Read pages 8 and 9

Purpose: to skim-read the section to find out what it will be about.

EXPLORE

Pause at page 9

Let's look at the heading on page 8. Why do you think the ice-cream has to be frozen?

Look at the drawing on page 8. How cold does the temperature have to be?

What are the arrows pointing to on page 9? Why do the workers have to wear earplugs? That's right, the machines are noisy in the packing area. How does the text show this? (*capital letters*)

READ

Read page 10

Purpose: to read the diagram and understand the process.

EXPLORE

Pause at page 10

What helped you to understand the diagram? (*reading the main text first*)

How many cartons are filled every minute?

Tricky word (page 10):
The word 'squirts' may be beyond the children's word recognition skills. Tell this word to the children.

Freezing

Then the ice cream goes through freezing pipes. The pipes are so cold that ice forms on them.

ice −7°C

Do not touch.

That makes the ice cream cold and soft. Yum!

8

Packing

Wear earplugs.
Too much noise.

Regular Flavours
Vanilla
Chocolate
Mint
Coffee
Lemon

In the packing area, the machines are very fast and VERY noisy. The workers have to wear earplugs. We had to wear earplugs too!

9

Watching the machines was fun.
One squirts the ice cream into cartons.

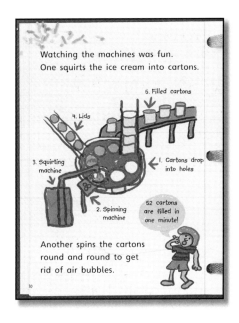

5. Filled cartons

4. Lids

3. Squirting machine

1. Cartons drop into holes

2. Spinning machine

52 cartons are filled in one minute!

Another spins the cartons round and round to get rid of air bubbles.

10

READ

Read pages 11 and 12

Purpose: to appreciate the difficulties of working in very cold temperatures.

EXPLORE

Pause at page 12

What is the title for this section?

Why do you think the children are hugging themselves? Why is there a drawing of someone in a thick coat?

Now read the text on your own and find out how cold it feels in the freezing room.

Why can't people wear contact lenses there?

READ

Read page 13

Purpose: to find out what happens to the ice-cream once it has been packed.

EXPLORE

Pause at page 13

What is the title of this section? What does it mean? (*Shipping.* Explain that to 'ship' goods now just means to transport them by road or rail. Once, when roads were bad, most transport over distance was by ship.)

Look at the photograph. Why is there a drawing of a cow on the side of the lorry?

What is special about these big trucks?

Hard Freezing

Finally, the ice cream is frozen solid in a very, very cold room. There is a machine that moves the air around. It is so cold it feels like 100° below zero in that room!

Cookie Flavours
Chocolate Chip
Cookies and Cream
Fudge Nut Brownie
Hot Fudge Brownie

11

Unusual Flavours
Ginger
Toffee Crunch
Tutti Frutti
Pistachio

It's so cold that the workers need to leave the freezer every 20 minutes to warm up. They can't wear contact lenses because they would stick to their eyes! Yuck! That's cold!

12

Shipping

Huge lorries take the ice cream to the shops. The trucks are like big freezers on wheels.

13

READ

Read pages 14 and 15

Purpose: to read and understand the flow chart.

EXPLORE

Pause at page 15

Let's look at the flow chart. What two things tell us what order to read the captions in? (*the arrows and the numbers*)

What do you notice about the shapes of the illustrations?

Now, read the captions on your own and find out what the flow chart is explaining.

Flowchart

1. Lorries bring milk to big tanks.

2. Milk is heated and made smooth.

3. Cream and sugar are added and stirred.

4. Flavours are added.

5. The ice cream goes through freezing pipes.

6. It is put into cartons.

7. It is frozen solid in a cold blast room.

8. Lorries take ice cream to the shops.

Follow-up

Independent Group Activity Work

Two photocopy masters, one with a reading focus and one with a writing focus, support the teaching objectives of this book.

The photocopy masters can be found in the Planning and Assessment Guide for Year 2.

PCM NF2.1 *(reading)*

PCM NF2.2 *(writing)*

You may also like to invite the children to read the text again during their independent reading (either at school or at home).

Writing

Guided writing: Draw a graph to represent the group's favourite ice-cream flavours. Label it and write an appropriate caption.

Extended writing: Using the flow chart on pages 14–15 as a model, ask the children to make a flow chart of a typical school day (e.g. starts with the register, lessons, break etc.).

Assessment Points

Assess that the children have learnt the main focus of the book by checking that they can:

- explain organisational features of texts, including layout, diagrams and captions.